CELTIC SONGS
with a Classical Flair

16 TRADITIONAL FOLK TUNES ARRANGED BY PHILLIP KEVEREN

— PIANO LEVEL —
INTERMEDIATE/LATE INTERMEDIATE

ISBN 978-1-5400-3263-8

HAL•LEONARD®

Visit Hal Leonard Online at
www.halleonard.com

Visit Phillip at
www.phillipkeveren.com

Contact Us:
Hal Leonard
7777 West Bluemound Road
Milwaukee, WI 53213
Email: info@halleonard.com

In Europe contact:
Hal Leonard Europe Limited
Distribution Centre, Newmarket Road
Bury St Edmunds, Suffolk, IP33 3YB
Email: info@halleonardeurope.com

In Australia contact:
Hal Leonard Australia Pty. Ltd.
4 Lentara Court
Cheltenham, Victoria, 3192 Australia
Email: info@halleonard.com.au

THE ASH GROVE

Old Welsh Air
Arranged by Phillip Keveren

THE BLUE BELLS OF SCOTLAND

Words and Music attributed to
MRS. JORDON
Arranged by Phillip Keveren

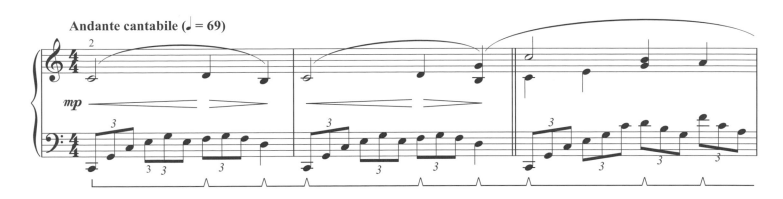

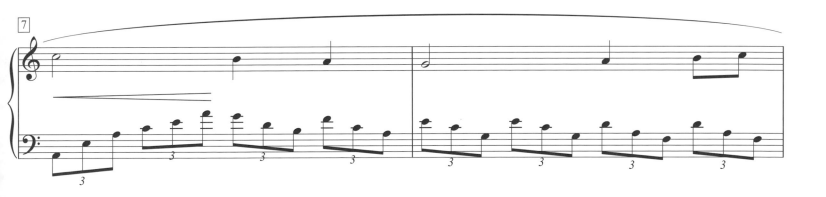

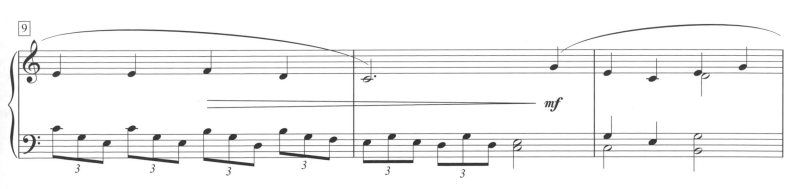

BARBARA ALLEN

Traditional English
Arranged by Phillip Keveren

COMIN' THROUGH THE RYE

Traditional Scottish Melody
Arranged by Phillip Keveren

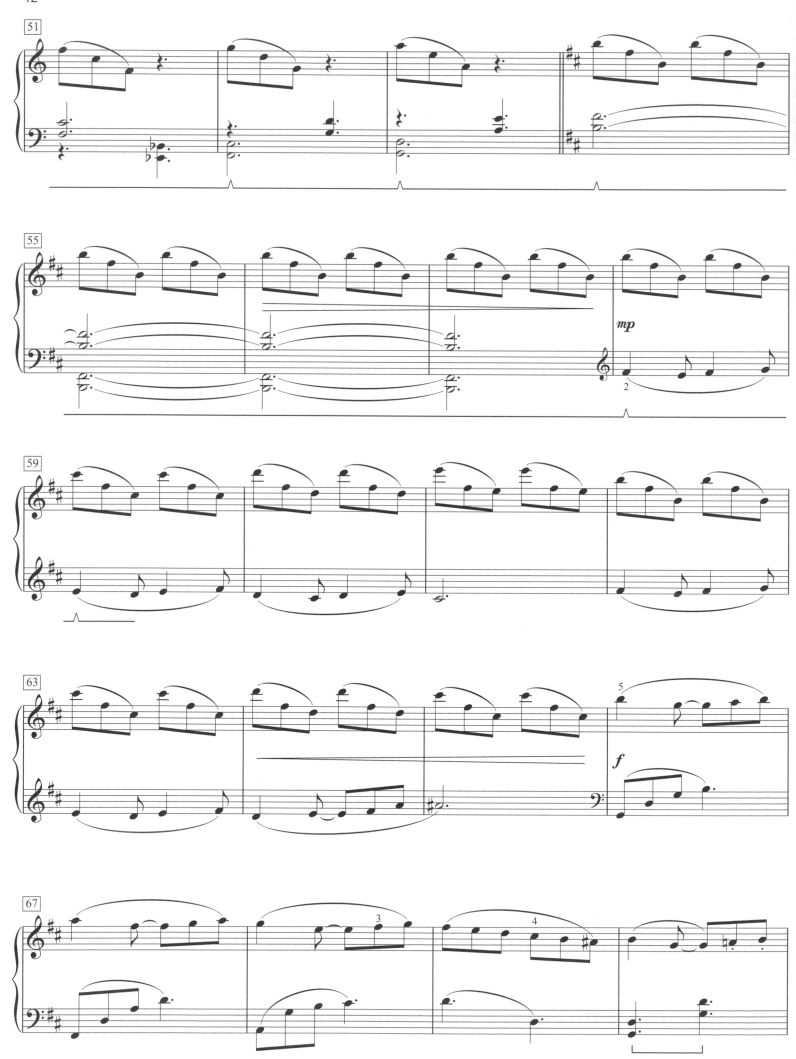

DOWN BY THE SALLEY GARDENS

Traditional Irish Folksong
Arranged by Phillip Keveren

FINNEGAN'S WAKE

Traditional Irish Folksong
Arranged by Phillip Keveren

A HIGHLAND LAD
MY LOVE WAS BORN

Traditional Scottish Melody
Arranged by Phillip Keveren

GARRYOWEN

Irish Folksong
Arranged by Phillip Keveren

THE IRISH ROVER

Traditional Irish Folksong
Arranged by Phillip Keveren

KERRY DANCE

By J.L. MOLLOY
Arranged by Phillip Keveren

LOCH LOMOND

Scottish Folksong
Arranged by Phillip Keveren

MOLLY MALONE
(Cockles & Mussels)

Irish Folksong
Arranged by Phillip Keveren

Jovial Waltz (♩ = 172)

THE RISING OF THE MOON

Traditional Irish Folksong
Arranged by Phillip Keveren

SKYE BOAT SONG

Traditional Scottish Melody
Arranged by Phillip Keveren

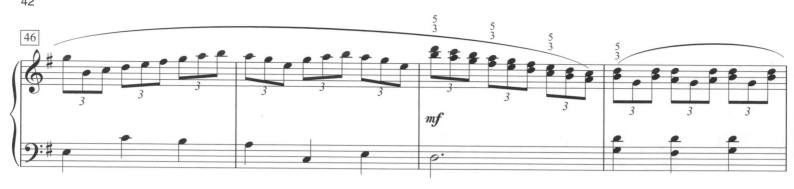

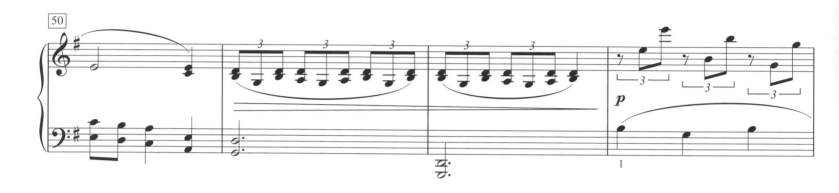

'TIS THE LAST ROSE OF SUMMER

Music by RICHARD ALFRED MILLIKEN
Arranged by Phillip Keveren

WILD ROVER

Traditional Irish Folksong
Arranged by Phillip Keveren